Verbs in Action
On the Run

Dana Meachen Rau

Marshall Cavendish
Benchmark
New York

Ready, set, go! The race is on.

Your arms and legs are pumping.
Your heart is beating fast.

You are running!

Children often run when they play.

Tag and baseball are running games.

People also run for *exercise*. Running makes your body strong.

Animals run, too. Some animals run from danger.

When a rabbit hears a dog bark, it runs! It runs to safety under a bush.

Some animals are *hunters*. They run to catch a meal.

The cheetah runs the fastest of all land animals. It hunts for zebras.

A river does not have legs. It does not need exercise. It does not chase after animals. But a river runs, too.

A river is a body of water. It is always moving.

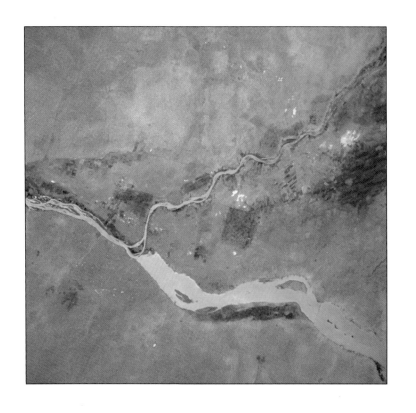

The Nile River is the longest river in the world. It runs a very long way through Africa.

Most rivers start in mountains. They run across the land.

Some rivers run into other rivers.

Rivers stop running when they reach the ocean.

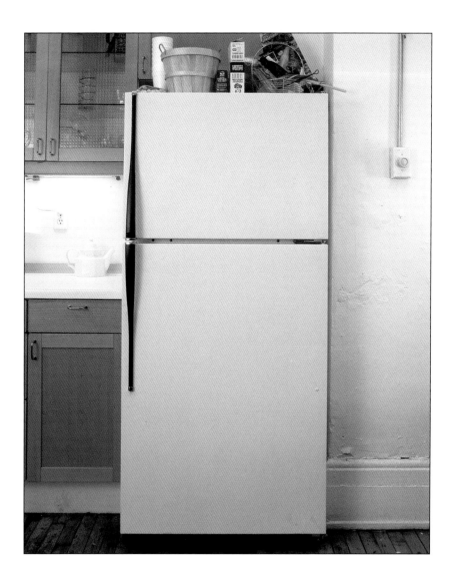

18

People use the word "run" to talk about machines, too.

A refrigerator runs. It does not race around your kitchen. It stays in one place. But the parts inside a refrigerator that make it work are moving.

Machines need *power*.

A car needs *gasoline*. Gasoline gives the car the power it needs to run.

21

Some machines plug into an *electrical outlet*. A vacuum cleaner gets power from electricity.

Some toys use *batteries* to give them power to run.

You may need a tissue if your
nose is running.

Have you ever hung up a painting before it was dry? The colors run into each other.

You might "run into" a friend at the park. Your father might tell you to "run along" when you leave for school.

If you feel tired, you might say
you feel "run down."

Running means something is on the move.

A person and a vacuum do not look the same. A rabbit and a river are very different. But they all have something in common. They can all run.

Challenge Words

batteries (BAT-uh-rees)—Small objects used to give power to small machines.

electrical outlet (i-LEK-tri-kuhl OUT-let)—The place where a machine gets electricity to make it run.

exercise (EK-suhr-size)—To do a lot of physical activity to keep your body healthy.

gasoline (gas-uh-LEEN)—A liquid that cars need to run.

hunters (HUN-tuhrs)—Animals that chase and eat other animals.

power (POW-uhr)—The energy machines need to run.

Index

Page numbers in **boldface** are illustrations.

With thanks to Nanci Vargus, Ed.D.
and Beth Walker Gambro, reading consultants

Marshall Cavendish Benchmark
Marshall Cavendish
99 White Plains Road
Tarrytown, New York 10591-9001
www.marshallcavendish.us

Library of Congress Cataloging-in-Publication Data

Rau, Dana Meachen, 1971–
On the run / by Dana Meachen Rau.
p. cm. — (Bookworms. Verbs in action)
Includes index.
ISBN 0-7614-1934-9
1. Run (The English word)—Juvenile literature. 2. English language—Verb—Juvenile literature.
I. Title II. Series: Rau, Dana Meachen, 1971– . Bookworms. Verbs in action.

PE1317.R86R38 2005
428.1—dc22
2004023397

Photo Research by Anne Burns Images

Cover photo: SuperStock/Stockbyte

The photographs in this book are used with permission and through the courtesy of: *Corbis*:
pp. 1, 9, 11 Tom Brakefield; p. 5 Bob Gomel; p. 12 Paul A. Souders; p. 14 Ron Watts; p. 17 David Muench;
pp. 22, 23, 25 Royalty Free; p. 29 Jim Cummins. *SuperStock*: p. 3 Delphine Fawundu; p. 4 Francisco Cruz;
p. 18 John Wilkes; p. 21 Stockbyte; p. 24 Pixtal; p. 26 Goodshoot; p. 27 ThinkStock. *Photri*: p. 6.
Photo Researchers: p. 15 NASA/Science Sources.

Series design by Becky Terhune

Printed in Malaysia
1 3 5 6 4 2